Written by KAREN COOLEY
Illustrated by TERRY JULIEN

Taken from Acts 16:16-34

A Jailer Is Set Free copyright © 2006 by Tyndale House Publishers, Inc., Carol Stream, Illinois 60188. All rights reserved. www.tyndale.com/kids. Originally published by Standard Publishing, Cincinnati, Ohio. First printing by Tyndale House Publishers, Inc., in 2013. Series design: Robert Glover. Cover and interior design: Steve Clark. *Happy Day* is a registered trademark of Tyndale House Publishers, Inc. The Tyndale Kids logo is a trademark of Tyndale House Publishers, Inc. For manufacturing information regarding this product, please call 1-800-323-9400.

ISBN 978-1-4143-9412-1

Printed in the United States of America

19	18	17	16	15	14	13
7	6	5	4	3	2	1

Paul and Silas loved God very much. They traveled to many different cities, teaching about Jesus and saying that he was the Son of God.

It was the same when they came to Philippi. Only this time, things turned out differently.

Everything was fine the first few days. Then Paul cast out an evil spirit in Jesus' name. This made some men really angry.

The angry men had Paul and Silas arrested, beaten, and thrown into my jail.

I put them inside their cell.
They were dangerous men, and I
had to be careful.

If they escaped, I would be blamed, so I checked twice to make sure their hands and feet were firmly chained.

Everything was very quiet . . . until right around midnight. That's when I heard something strange. I crept through the dark halls of the jail, looking and listening.

It was Paul and Silas! They were in their cell, chained up tight, singing at the top of their lungs. And they were happy! I had never seen anything like this before. They sat singing and praying while the other prisoners leaned in close to listen. They had to be crazy!

Suddenly, the ground began to shake.
My legs wobbled under me. All around, I could
hear walls crumbling and metal crashing.

Then my feet flew out from under me! I was terrified!

Finally, it stopped. I looked around at the crumbled jail. What a mess! Going inside a cell, I saw loose chains lying all over the floor. Where were Paul and Silas? Were the other prisoners gone? What was I going to do? My life was ruined!

As I picked up my sword to end my life, a voice stopped me. "Don't harm yourself! We're all here!"

Quickly, I dropped the chains and looked around to see who had spoken.

It was Paul. I couldn't believe it! He was right. Every prisoner was still there. No one had left the crumbled jail after the earthquake.

That's when I knew Paul and Silas were men of God. These things that happened—the singing, the earthquake, the prisoners not escaping—they were truly amazing. I wanted to know this powerful God they served.

"How can I be saved?" I asked, kneeling in front of them. They told me to believe in the Lord Jesus Christ and I would be saved. From that point on, I believed.

I took Paul and Silas to my home where I washed their wounds. Then I asked them to baptize me and everyone in my family. What a wonderful experience! Jesus was my Savior! Joy filled my heart and I felt like singing. My life was changed. This jailer was set free!